The Way of the Couch

To Patty –
To paraphrase your
bumper sticker –
um, This Happened.

Regards,

Andy

The Way of the Couch

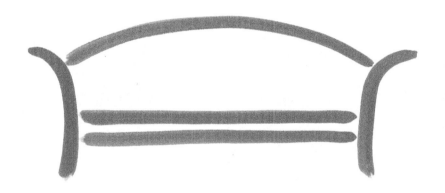

A Spiritual Guide

for Binge Watchers and Beer Drinkers

By

A.P. Beemer

For Thomas and Patrick

Introduction

Life will wear you out.
It is easy to forget how to relax
when you are racing around all day
like a drunken ferret.

It would be good to have
the wisdom of a Chinese Master,
the serenity of a Zen monk,
the presence of Caine from "Kung Fu."

We all know how.

But the ways of the Eastern mystic
are strange to Western ears.

We require the wisdom
of the East in the language
of the American family room.

1

There was something strong and forgiving
before this house was ever built.
It stood alone, silent and unchanging.
It has been here forever,
and because I know no better name
I call it the couch.

Its great spirit flows from the cushions
like beer from an over-pumped keg
and fills every room of the house
but leaves not a single beer stain.

The couch is great.
The TV is great.
The fridge is great.
The king and queen of the house are great.

The king and queen go to the fridge.
The fridge is full of products from the TV.
The TV is placed in front of the couch.
The couch is a force of nature.

<u>2</u>

The couch that can be described
is not the softest couch.
The nap that can be disturbed
is not the nap eternal.

Sit on the sofa and know
napping is the beginning of living in peace.
Sink into the cushions and consider:
what do you want?

Wanting only the couch
leaves you free to observe the television.
Wanting more than the couch
obscures even the beer in your grasp

Realize wanting and not wanting
grow from the same confusing notions.
Once you have cleared your beery mind,
you have opened the door to comprehending the couch.

<u>3</u>

Can you stop fidgeting and switching channels
and park your mind on just one thing?

Can you loaf on the cushions
like a baby dozes in its crib?
Can you wipe the brewer's haze
from your eyes
and find the remote?
Can you open the fridge
without forcing the Falstaff on guests?

Do you have clear sight lines to the telly?
Can you stop short of judging the new fall lineup?

The couch is used best by codgers and toddlers.
They surrender to it, though it makes no demands.
They doze lazily and it does not mock them.
It is the seat of perfect relaxation.

<u>4</u>

The Master is pleased
with any evening's entertainment.
He welcomes guests who sit quietly
and sip carefully.
Likewise, he welcomes those who guzzle,
holler, and knock over the pretzels.
This is proof of his true kindness.

The Master is an enigma,
and though he is hard to read
like newspaper in a bird cage,
when he speaks he makes us all
feel like children at Christmas.

5

Frayed and lumpy, the couch
seems eternal because
its date of manufacture is obscure.
Friendly and loyal, it waits humbly
for the heft of your lounging rear.

The Master seems to lag;
that is why she is two steps ahead.
She seems not to care;
that is how she achieves leisure immersion.
The Master wants only one thing -
that is why she is always contented.

<u>6</u>

The couch is the center of the household,
the resting place of the laborer,
the consolation of the unemployed.

A good word can get you a job.
A good deed can keep the neighbors friendly.
If these things are so easily bought,
how much are they worth?

When a new boss arrives,
don't flatter him or do him favors.
Tell him to take a nap.

Once you harness the power in the pillows,
what you seek in life, you find,
and what you screw up, you are forgiven.
That's why the cushioned wonder
has been worshiped since antiquity.

7

The potato planted on the couch cannot be uprooted.
The tomato holding tightly cannot fall.
Generations will honor her as the tenacious, lazy one.

Park your rear on the couch and live honestly.
Stack the family across the cushions and prosper.
Seat the neighbors on the armrests and grow close.
Pile the whole town on top and be drunk with joy.

Want to know how it all works?
Watch carefully.

<u>8</u>

For now,
think about nothing -
rest your spinning brain.
Watch the sports fans go mad
and know it will happen again.

Every rump in the house
wants to rest on a couch.
This is clear and simple:
If you don't understand the couch
you will be a wondering sluggard
but when you truly understand
you will be tolerant
and walk with a silly grin,
you will be kind as Grandma
and move with royal dignity.

Once you know the way of the couch
every day will be Super Bowl Sunday,
and when the game is over you will grin
and be eager for the start of spring training.

9

The highest form is cold beer;
it is tasty and refreshing to everyone.
There are brands for all,
even those who have little.

The best living room is any comfortable place.
The greatest ads are understood by all.
The remote is best handled with quick fingers of justice.
For maximum cheer, take turns shagging beer.

When couch-bound and still,
rest your feet and swill a brew.
When couch time is through, enjoy yourself
as if you were still on the couch.
There is a time to sit, and a time to move.

10

Allow TV fools to loom like gods
and honest people will seem small and dull.
Believe the lies in ads
and you will lust after cheap plastic gadgets.

Were the Master President
she would empty the nation of worry
and load the fridges with refreshments,
empty the offices on weekends
and fill the dens with workers reclining.

She would cause families
to lose the TV Guide but
be content in not knowing
what shows come next.

If everyone could relax on the couch
for a while, the world would be just fine.

11

The Master knows the couch deeply;
his understanding is amazing.
We can't express it ourselves;
we only say he naps all the time.

He is difficult to describe, this loafer:
watchful as a receiver on a crossing pattern,
shy as a flatulent guest,
changing like the ice around a keg,
cool as a fresh-fluffed pillow,
welcoming as a worn recliner,
clear as digital reception.

Can you wait for the bubbles to rise
and the glass to clear before you drink?
Can you postpone the celebration
until the team has won?

The Master makes no effort to be satisfied.
He avoids senseless prediction,
and he is happy with whatever comes along.

12

A happy man is easy to find,
A recent error is easy to fix,
A glass bottle is easy to shatter,
A few small crumbs are easy to scatter.

Scrub the dishes before they fill the sink.
Quiet the fans before they swing their fists.

Every tree in the forest
started with a tiny seed.
Every house in the neighborhood
started with a pile of logs.
Every trip to the fridge
starts with a single step from the couch.

Rising too fast, you grow dizzy and fall.
Grasping desperately, you drop the ball.

13

Change channels without lifting a finger,
mow the lawn without moving.
Regard the portable as a big-screen,
regard a six-pack as a fridgeful.
Do the dirty work before things get dirty,
divide one tough job into many quick tasks.

Someone who will agree to anything
is unreliable.
Someone who thinks everything is easy
is forever facing difficulty.

The Master knows this.
The Master doesn't
seek greatness --
she is just
great.

<u>14</u>

The glutton who gobbles pizza grows ill.
The fool who guzzles whiskey falls flat.
The life of the party has few true friends.
The consummate fan is a consummate boob.
The clod who hoards the remote will be
unhappy with every channel.

Insist upon this excess and you will
suffer the lumps of a fall from the couch.

Avoid such excess and you will
find splendor on the sofa.

15

Happy babies are soft and pink.
Dead bodies are hard and stiff.
Fresh-sprouted grass is green and bending.
Dying trees are gray and dry.

Those who are stiff
and inflexible soon crack.
Those who are soft
and flexible stay strong.

In the end,
Hardness will shatter like a beer bottle.
Softness will last like a couch cushion.

16

Taking it easy is easy,
but fools like to make life hard.
Don't turn first and goal into third and long,
and remember to recline.

See,
when a corporate clod buys half of Nebraska,
but Uncle Ned hasn't space for a garden,
or when Senator Dingbat chops at a tee box
while millions holler and moan,

when stew-eyed lawyers stir misfortune into gravy,
these are all signs that the couch has been forgotten.

The Master doesn't control the remote;
therefore she has control.
Uncle Ned must have the remote;
therefore he has no control.

The Master watches nothing,
yet nothing is left unwatched.
Uncle Ned watches everything he can,
yet he can never watch everything.

A decent man switches channels,
but all shows seem the same.
A fair man switches channels,
still all shows are the same.
A moral man switches channels,
and when he finds a show distasteful,
he makes a fist and threatens the network.

When the couch is forgotten, people are courteous.
When courtesy is forgotten, people tolerate one another.
When tolerance is forgotten, people do what laws require.
But laws are like TV: turn them off,
and there is nothing there.
So,
the Master reacts to reality,
not to soap operas.
She appreciates the comfort of the living room,
not the appearance.

<u>18</u>

Shake a full beer and it will foam --
better to keep it still.
Switch channels too often and
the remote will break.
Lust for a big-screen TV and
your heart will wither watching smaller.
Boast of your sporting greatness
and all will think you a liar and a fool.

You must learn that happiness is not a competition;
this is the first step to the peace of the couch.

<u>19</u>

The return of the weekend completes
the cycle of the couch.
Surrender to slumber is
the way of the couch.

All things are started from resting,
and resting is defined by periods
of not resting.

20

Raising a family is like grilling thin steak:
too much heat and you'll burn it up.

Head the household towards the sofa
and laughter will rule.
Little Timmy and Baby Davey will crash and tumble,
but they'll always get up giggling.

When nobody fights,
everyone gains.

21

Knowing when Uncle Ned is pickled
is a kind of brilliance.
Knowing when to end your own brew swigging
is real wisdom.

Stopping Uncle Ned from driving the Chrysler
is a kind of strength.
Stopping yourself from weaving to the beer store
is real power.

If you know that you have enough,
you have real wealth.
If you remain poised when others panic,
you will prosper.

22

Football or friendship -- which is more worthy?
Hockey or teeth -- which makes you wealthy?
Beer or pizza -- which is less healthy?

Realize that each beer you drink
will pad your ponderous gut.
Realize that for each extra peso
you will surrender something precious.

Be content with what comes your way
and you'll never regret your choices.
Be satisfied with today
and enjoy a long, healthy life.

23

If you make foolish bets, your regrets
will last as long as a Super Bowl halftime.
Don't blame others for your stupid schemes.
Just don't be stupid.

For this reason,
the Master buys his own beer
and shags his own pretzels.
He minds his own business
and lets others mind theirs.

24

The way of the couch is like a ballpark hot dog:
the outside is soft, the inside substantial.

Those who complicate the dog,
who offer footlongs and turkey brats,
have lost all sense of the couch.
They try to improve what was
perfect and sufficient already.

The Master honors the dog's tubular perfection.
He burns the meat flawlessly
without timers or formulas,
always aware that his grill work
can make the dog worse,
but never better.

25

A proper beer run has no real purpose.
A perfect plate of nachos has no recipe.
A worthy cable man will search deeply
to remove obstacles to pure reception.

Likewise the Master welcomes all,
even twits, without judgment.
He produces sweet beer from brine,
burgers from brambles.
He wastes nothing.

In this way the Master loses not
an evening's pleasure, ever.

Those who are happy must lead the boring.
The boring exist to challenge the happy.
If this is unclear to you,
you will suffer a thousand maddening days;
this is what life is all about.

26

The power of the couch flows everywhere.
Though it supplies the will to mow
the lawn and wash the truck before kickoff
it does not boast of its strength.

Sluggards arise from the couch with drive
yet the couch appears to contain no energy.
Because it seems empty,
we call the couch a humble seat.
But because it provides eternal retreat,
we know the couch is truly great.

<u>27</u>

Was the couch already placed
before you bought the house?
A home starts with the couch's position,
and a family finds the way to it.

Decide the winner
before the game is played
and seek to soak the bookie;
your heart will stammer and race.
Plop down on the couch
and just watch the game;
the throbbing will dwindle.

Clear vision in a shit storm is brilliance.
Surrender as strategy is strength.
See with your own eyes
and make up your own mind.
That will keep you busy enough.

<u>28</u>

Who can distinguish between an ad and the nightly news?
Who draws distinctions between turkey dogs and T-bones?
Why care about the tastes of other?
Why do what they do?
It's like chasing a squirrel.

Many people get excited
about Super Bowl Sunday.
Only the Master remains calm and blank,
like a fat, happy baby
or Uncle Ned dozing after dinner.

Everyone wants more stuff.
Only the Master is happy
without a big screen, content
to let his mind roam and forget.

Everyone wants to seem smart.
The Master confesses he doesn't know much.
The Master isn't sure what's up next;
he floats through channels
like a dry leaf in a gusting breeze.

Of course, he's strange --
he enjoys things the way they are.

Inside each old, fat man is a thin, young man.
From lounging comes the vitality to do great deeds.

In similar fashion the Master voyages afar
without leaving the giant recliner.
No matter how alarming the nightly news
he remains calmly himself.
Witnessing this composure, why deny
another the opportunity to recline?

The Master remembers:
when the game is over it will be time
to insist on the painting of shutters.
But should the nagging begin
before the final horn sounds,
it will be clear who has lost the way.

<u>30</u>

Big words disguise the truth;

the truth is neither distant nor complex.

The network expert is no genius.

The true genius doesn't claim to be expert.

The Master needs few things in life.

The more help she provides,

the more gets.

The more she gives away,

the more she has.

Thus,

The couch way is comfortable.

The Master shows the way

without shoving.

31

Living in peace with the couch
the family room is uncluttered,
the fridge is full,
and the tribe breathes easily,
accepting each other's tastes in tube
and growing up strong together.

If one interferes with the cycle of rest,
the family room piles with papers,
the fridge empties, and the tribe,
howling and shrieking,
disbands.

Therefore,
a wise man knows it is best
to be humble upon the couch.
He does not seek praise,
neither too high after a win
nor too low after loss.

He likes the middle road,
not bubbly as champagne,
nor flat as day-old beer.

32

When the Master wields the remote
no one notices she has it.
Not as good is the remote-holder
whose shows are tolerated.
Next worst is the channel-swapper everyone fears,
and worst is the one whose frantic switching is hated.

If the remote keeper doesn't trust the selections of others,
no one will trust him with the remote.

The Master chooses channels carefully.
She does her work quietly
and everyone, amazed, says,
"Look at what we have done."

33

Eliminate network experts and televangelists
and the den will be washed in TV's warm, loving glow.

Abolish rules and manners
and the family will share the chips and soda.

Decrease greed
and it's doughnut time for cops.

This sounds too simple
but everything is simple
when you are relaxed.

Unwind on the couch,
and watch the world turn out fine.

34

When the path to the beer is open,
consumption is joyous and moderate.
When the road to sudsville is closed,
the hoarding and guzzling are rampant.

When the fridge runs dry,
Uncle Ned hides cans under cushions,
and his kind eyes go beer-skewed.

Great drunkenness is apparent to the sober.
Sobriety is the fleeting absence of intoxication.
Who knows what the desperate will drink?

To avoid beer trouble, it is important to be
moderate but not miserly,
direct but not insulting,
honest but not angry.

35

Search for the last beer and you won't find it.
Listen for the cap's gasp and you won't hear it.
Grab for its cold neck and you'll grab air.
Use your senses as one and find the last beer.

You won't see the bottle cap smiling above the pickle jar.
You won't see the label peeking between milk and mustard.

The last bottle is not to be found
yet everyone has it already in hand.
It refreshes everyone
though no one has guzzled.

Open the bottle and find no beer.
Pour out the beer and see no foamy head.

This may seem mysterious
but when you stop straining to understand
you will be on the way to understanding.

36

Do you have a plan to rearrange the living room?
Know that these schemes often fail.

The living room is a sacred space,
and not a candidate for improvement.
Start moving furniture and you may break it,
or worse, destroy sight lines to the TV.

Among sports fans,
some cheer for the Red Sox,
others pray for the Cubbies;
some watch games slack-jawed,
other holler at the tube;
some jump and thrash at each play,
others doze in the cathode twilight;
some change allegiance in a hostile crowd,
others persevere and suffer.

Know that the Master
avoids severe habits,
rejects extreme policies,
and remains the cooler head that prevails.

37

Clear reception may appear snowy,
yet yields useful pictures.
A full beer may feel empty,
yet contains enough suds to satisfy.

The thickest carpet feels threadbare,
the funniest joke seems pointless,
the best meal tastes like nothing at all.

When you are cold, move.
When you are hot, rest.
Do what must be done,
and keep it simple.

38

If you want an oil can of brew,
drink half a can.
If you propose to stretch out on the sofa,
curl up in a ball.
If you hunger for charcoaled flesh,
put down your burger.
If you want to wake up,
dig into the pillow.
If you require a relaxing day,
arise and mow the lawn.

The Master reclines peacefully
and provides an accidental example.
Because he disavows image,
we see his power.

Believe this:
if you want a relaxing Saturday
mowing the lawn is good medicine.
Once you know the couch,
your old notions don't much matter.

39

To believe some couches beautiful,
you must condemn others as ugly.
To rate some couches comfortable,
you must feel others' lumps and springs.

Good TV and bad TV pay for each other.
Long couches and short love seats measure each other.
High hassocks and low tables both hold a bowl of chips.
Ads after one show and before the next
form the ancient continuum.

Because of these truths,
the Master flips channels in perfect time, silently.
Programs flicker and he sits sleepily;
programs disappear and he remains peaceful.
When his couch time is done, he arises
without regrets, and forever
regards the couch fondly.

40

The stadium is a monster of steel and concrete
but the expanse inside the cavern
is where the game is won or lost.

The den is arranged around the TV
but it is from the couch
that the family cheers.

We ponder the hardness of a beer bottle
but it is the emptiness inside
that makes the bottle useful.

It seems that hard, apparent things are useful,
but it is in empty spaces that life resides.

41

Realize that all things come and go,
and smile at your show's final episode.
If you're not afraid of endings,
you won't be afraid of durings.

When the big screen starts burning,
don't call the plumber.
If the disk stops its turning,
go for a walk.

42

When a great man discovers the couch
he stretches out and becomes part of it.
When Uncle Ned hears of its powers
he scratches his belly and sniffs the air.
When the foolish sluggard hears of the couch
he laughs like hell.

So, the saying goes:
the bright flicker from the TV appears dark,
the way to the fridge leads back to the couch,
the kitchen floor, once level, feels sloped,
TV breasts are perfect, but plastic,
loyal fan support disappears overnight,
and the smallest kids have the biggest answers.

Things are rarely as they seem to be --
much is concealed in the cushions of the couch.

43

The parent who respects the weight of the couch
doesn't try to shove the kids off it.
Shoving the little buggers
only makes them stubborn.
A militant stance results in militant children.

The Master applies discipline
but goes no further.
He knows that ultimately
the offspring go their own way
and trying to force that way
will drive the family from the couch.
Secure in his ability,
he needs not boast to children.
Comfortable in his appearance,
he ignores teens laughing at his socks.
Able to admit his faults,
his authority is respected.

Those who have fallen from the couch
turn into scowling cranks;
such refusal to unclench
results in four-chambered misfortune.

44

Let the family be friendly,
and respect the power of lot lines.
Let the family value good living
and be satisfied in their home.

Let the kids have Playstation
but no urge to abuse it.
Let the father have butcher knives,
the mother a chain saw,
and let them wield these wisely.

Let the family burn burgers with the neighbors.
So let their burgers be juicy,
their egg salad cold,
their chips crunchy,
and their weekends happy.

Though they know strange and wonderful places
are but a cramped flight away,
let them be content if they never travel,
and when it is their time,
let them go peacefully.

45

The wisest coach never screams,
the true champion doesn't taunt,
the dominant athlete competes with history,
the team captain works for the team.

Play fair,
respect your rival:
this truth is older than television.

46

All sport provides the opportunity for mayhem,
yet the superior sportsman avoids using
the equipment as a weapon.

The batter who charges the mound
has lost his mind.
The linebacker who tackles with his helmet
is already addled.
The winger who swings his stick like a hatchet
skates like a hatful of assholes.

Why cheer a big hit,
but stand in sorrow
when a player crumbles?

Start with the knowledge that it's only a game,
and do not cheer too wildly over victories.

47

Winning is as dangerous as losing.
Hoping for a win is as useless as fearing a loss.

Why is winning as dangerous as losing?
Win or lose,
the game hinges on chance.
Be unconcerned with winning and losing;
the twists in your beery stomach will unwind.

Why is hoping as useless as fearing?
Hope and fear don't get you off the couch
nor let you relax on the couch.
Let loose of hope and fear.
Forget about outcomes
and your clogged brain will clear.

Spread the snacks across the living room.
Disregard pretzels in the pillows
and the newspaper underfoot.
Enjoy it as it is
and you'll be ready to clean up
when the game is over.

48

A quick swing of the stick gets you one.
A hard tackle in the end zone gets you two.
Between the uprights gets you three.
Three strikes and you're out.

Some folks won't share
the hooch and hot dogs,
and make hoarding
and guzzling a contest.
Stop their ceaseless feed
and we'll all feast like kings.

Everyone wants to be on the tube,
yet celebrities want to be left
alone.

See through this fog and film,
find a clearer picture,
and show someone.

49

The flashing color screen makes us blind.
The stereo sound makes us deaf.
A diet of frozen pizza fills our arteries.
Lust for gadgets shrinks our souls.
Two-hundred channels confuse our minds.

Because of this,
the Master believes in herself
and trusts her intuition.

50

The couch is impartial;
it accepts pillows, pets, and people.
The Master is also impartial;
he will relax with simpletons and sovereigns.

The couch is an immense pillow;
its squishy welcome is obvious.
The more the couch is used,
the softer its greeting
and the deeper its
relaxation.

Even a sagging, ancient couch
will cradle your tired bones.

51

Some find these words ridiculous.
Others call them useless
But only because it is strange
is this teaching useful.

If my teaching was normal,
it would cause fist fights and chest pain,
like everything else.

The important stuff is simple:
Be good-natured at game time,
and your cheers will be met with humor.
Be cautious in consumption,
and you can spare a guest a beer.
Be gracious in victory,
and you will be respected in defeat.

About the Author

A.P. Beemer was born in Niagara Falls, Canada in 1967
and educated at the University of Michigan.
He enjoyed careers in engineering and aircraft preservation
before opting to stay home with the kids.
He lives in Nebraska with one wife,
two sons, and three couches.

Made in the USA
Monee, IL
08 June 2020